LEONARDO DA VINCI

Renaissance Man

THE HISTORY HOUR

Copyright © 2018 by Kolme Korkeudet Oy

All rights reserved.

No part of this book may be reproduced in any form or by any electronic or mechanical means, including information storage and retrieval systems, without written permission from the author, except for the use of brief quotations in a book review.

CONTENTS

PART I
Introduction 1

PART II
Early Life 5

PART III
Apprenticeship with Verrocchio, 1466-76 7

PART IV
Leonardo, Master of his Craft 11

PART V
Mastery of Chiaroscuro 15

PART VI
Working in Milan, 1482-99 17

PART VII
The Virgin of the Rocks 19

PART VIII
The Last Supper 23

PART IX
Other Projects 29

PART X
Human Anatomy 33

PART XI
Flight from Milan 37

PART XII
Return to Florence 41

PART XIII
Military Engineer for Cesare Borgia (1502-03) . . 45

PART XIV
The Battle of Anchiaro 51

PART XV
Sojourn in Milan (1506-08) 55

PART XVI
Rome (1513-16) 59

PART XVII
Michelangelo and Leonardo   61

PART XVIII
Final Years   65

PART XIX
Leonardo's Verifiable Paintings   69

PART XX
Leonardo's Private Life   77

PART XXI
How Can We Use Leonardo's Strengths In Our
Lives?   83

PART XXII
Additional Reading List   87

Your Free eBook!   89

I
INTRODUCTION

On April 15th of 1452, Caterina, a sixteen-year-old serving girl, working for a notary name Piero in the town of Vinci in the region of Florence (modern day Tuscany) gave birth, out of wedlock, to a son they named Leonardo. Although this young boy would go on to become the most recognized example of the "**Renaissance man**" in the sense that he achieved great things in the areas of Renaissance painting and sculpture, architecture, science, music, mathematics, engineering, cartography, astronomy, geology, botany, human anatomy, history, and many other areas, he was not born to any great lord or famous artist. He was known, during his lifetime, as Leonardo, di ser Piero da Vinci, which in the fashion of the time would translate to Leonardo, of the nobleman Piero, who comes from Vinci.

Uncharacteristically, for the time, he traveled quite widely, and worked in many disparate subject areas, because he did not really consider himself to be primarily a painter, even though he is best remembered today as the painter of two of the most critical pieces of renaissance art, the *Mona Lisa* (*La Gioconda*) and *The Last Supper*. In fact, when he wrote a letter requesting employment to Ludovico il moro Sforza, Duke of Milan, he only added that he was a painter and sculptor as a sort of postscript, emphasizing his skills as a maker of offensive and defensive weapons, and as an architect. His reasons for doing this are many and various, but also, they were determined by the fashion and priorities of the time. Mainly though it was because he did not want to be pigeon-holed as a painter; knowing that it was a time of war, he wanted to be known as a creator of new implements of war. Never mind the fact that he had never created a weapon in his life!

The 1400s were a time when gunpowder was being widely experimented with in war, and many of the warlike rulers of the principalities of northern Italy were interested in getting a better weapon than their neighbor, thereby giving them more relative power in the region. Leonardo was well aware of this and saw the place of art within this society as secondary; it would be wrong to assume that Leonardo himself did not value his abilities.

According to Giorgio Vasari, the author of the first definitive book on renaissance artists, *The Lives of the Artists*, Leonardo was both extremely attractive, talented in virtually every area, an exceptionally good orator, singer, and debater. He was frequently described as peculiar by Vasari though, and it is difficult to know for sure what this really means. Clearly, he had some strange attributes: he was left-handed at a time when this was not widely accepted as appropriate (which may account for the peculiar mirror writing that he used for his private notebooks), he was gay at a time when it was not only socially unacceptable but illegal (he was charged with '**sodomy**' in 1476, but acquitted, according to Florentine legal records), and he was a free thinker at a time when northern Italian society was extremely stratified. As a person who did not fit into any of the conventional molds of renaissance society, he was free to move between the classes and free to do what he liked within his own society.

ஃ

Interestingly, for a person who was so prolific despite his apparent inability to finish projects, there are only a handful of paintings that can definitively be attributed to Leonardo's hand. These include the angel in Verrocchio's *The Baptism of Christ*, the two paintings of *The Annunciation* (the first in the Uffizi, and the second in the Louvre), *The Adoration of the Magi* (in the Hermitage in St Petersburg), *St. Jerome* (in the Vatican), the two *Madonna of the Rocks* (in the British Museum and the Louvre), *The Last Supper* in Milan, and the *Mona Lisa*, *St John the Baptist* (both of which are in the Louvre), and *Salvator Mundi*. No major painter in the world is known so well by so few works. And so, in one of the starkest examples of quality and not quantity, we are about to embark on a journey through the known life and work of the world's greatest creative genius, examining many of the lesser known facts of his creative and personal life.

II
EARLY LIFE

"Painting is poetry that is seen rather than felt, and poetry is painting that is felt rather than seen."

— LEONARDO DA VINCI

He was born out of wedlock into a fairly strict, regimented, and stratified society in the Florentine town of Vinci in the lower valley of the Arno River, to a father, a notary with some social standing and with descendants who were noble, named Piero Fruosino di Antonio da Vinci, and a mother who was a peasant girl named Caterina. Leonardo seems to have spent his first five years living with his mother in her hometown, the small hamlet of Anchiano.

Little is known of his early life because of this, although he seems to have lived comfortably and relatively happily until 1457 when he was five years old, at which point he moved in with his father in Vinci.

※

His father lived in the family house with his brother and father, and also with his new sixteen-year-old bride, Albiera Amadori who was very kind to Leonardo but who died young in 1465 without having had any children.

※

According to Giorgio Vasari, Leonardo studied languages, mathematics, and music during his youth, and he was so adept at all three that he could have made a career in any of them. He studied mathematics so profoundly that the questions Leonardo asked he constantly stumped his own teacher. When he studied music, he was recognized widely for having a beautiful singing voice, and his skill on the lute was so great that he was invited to perform for the Duke of Milan. When he traveled there at the behest of the Duke of Florence, he arrived with a lute he had made by himself out of bronze that was in the shape of a horse's head, which was so beautiful that he outdid all the other musicians in the Milanese court. (This was quite a feat since the court of the Sforzas had been known as one of the finest in Europe for polyphonic secular song). Leonardo also presented the horse's head lute to the duke along with a letter seeking employment. This letter, which has been frequently quoted because of its emphasis on his abilities as a designer of implements of war, noted that he was a painter and sculptor too, but only as an afterthought.

III
APPRENTICESHIP WITH VERROCCHIO, 1466-76

"A painter should begin every canvas with a wash of black, because all things in nature are dark except where exposed by the light."

— LEONARDO DA VINCI

※

Leonardo's father, Piero, was a close friend with Andrea di Cione, known as Verrocchio, and when he saw the beautiful drawings his son had created, he sought out Verrochio's advice on what to do with his career, thinking that he would excel at design. Verrocchio was so impressed with his drawings that he agreed to take him on, at the age of fourteen, into his workshop. Here he was exposed to many of the skills that he later perfected, including drafting, chemistry, metallurgy and metalwork, leatherwork, drawing, painting and sculpting, plaster casting, architecture, mechanics, and carpentry.

❦

His time in the workshop of Verrocchio was of typical methods used at the time to train the great masters, and he was joined in this workshop by other young apprentices who would go on to be great masters themselves, including Ghirlandaio, Botticelli, and Perugino among others. The way this studio would work was that the master, Verrocchio, would get a commission and plan the work. He would complete the key parts of the painting and leave the secondary areas, the background, the secondary figures, and so on to the apprentices.

❦

According to Vasari, when Verrocchio was commissioned to paint a panel depicting St John baptizing Christ, (the painting depicted below is called *The Baptism of Christ*), Leonardo was tasked to paint an angel holding Christ's garments. The depiction of garments was highly prized because of the play of light on the folds, and when Leonardo painted his angel, Verrocchio was so impressed with his knowledge of the *chiaroscuro* style including the play of light and shade on the angel and the cloth that herefused to paint in colour anymore, declaring that his young apprentice was more adept than he was. Close examination of the painting reveals that it was originally painted in tempera with touch-ups using the new technique of oil paint, and, according to experts, many of the rocks around the brown mountain stream in the painting, as well as much of the figure of Christ, reveal the hand of Leonardo.

Whether or not Verrocchio ever painted again is a matter of myth more than a matter of fact, but the point is that Leonardo did qualify as a master soon after, in 1472, when he was only twenty when he was admitted to the Accademia of St. Luke. Nevertheless, he continued to collaborate with Verrocchio for several more years, even likely being the model for several works by the master, including the bronze statue of *David* (below) and the angel Gabriel in the painting called *Tobias and the Angel*, both by Verrocchio. Both of these figures depict a singularly attractive young man.

❧ IV ☙
LEONARDO, MASTER OF HIS CRAFT

"Once you have tasted flight, you will forever walk the earth with your eyes turned skyward, for there you have been, and there you will always long to return."

— LEONARDO DA VINCI

Leonardo left the workshop of Verrocchio in 1476, even

though he had begun his professional career as early as August 5, 1473, with his first signed pen and ink drawing of the Arno Valley.

Misfortune struck him in the first year of his professional career in 1476 when he, along with three other young men, was charged by the Florentine authorities with sodomy. Even though he was acquitted when no witnesses came forward, he did not produce anything for two years, and it is suspected that he must have feared for his life.

※

By 1478, he had officially left Verrocchio's workshop, and he no longer lived with his father. One contemporary writer claimed that he was living in the palace of the ruling Medici family, and working in the neo-Platonic academy called the Giardino of the Piazza San Marco.

※

There is another possible apocryphal tale about Leonardo that is very telling of his skill as a chiaroscuro painter. It is told that he was living in rented rooms in Florence, and his landlady asked him to pay the rent. Unable to come up with the money, he promised her that he would have the money soon and that he would use his closet filled with priceless garments as collateral. He then painted the inside of an empty closet so perfectly that when he showed it to her, she agreed to let him stay until he got the money. While this is a romantic and probably untrue story, it does illustrate the power of Leonardo's skill as a painter.

※

Even though he spent a great deal of time on other projects while living in Florence, he did get several lucrative commissions. Early in 1478, he received a commission to paint an altarpiece for the chapel of San Bernardo in the Palazzo Vecchio, the Florentine city hall. According to researcher Jack Wasserman, he also received another commission to paint an *Adoration of the Magi* for the monks of San Donato a Scopeto. Typically, of Leonardo, neither commission was completed. *The Adoration of the Magi* was interrupted when he was invited by the great patron Lorenzo de' Medici to go to the court of Ludovico 'il moro' Sforza, the Duke of Milan. It was at this visit that he brought with him the lute in the shape of a horse's head that he had fashioned out of bronze, and his oft-quoted letter itemizing his skills in making war implements and adding, almost as an afterthought, that he could also paint:

> *"I can create sculptures in marble, bronze, or clay and I can also paint whatever may be needed."*

V
MASTERY OF CHIAROSCURO

"Study without desire spoils the memory, and it retains nothing that it takes in."

— LEONARDO DA VINCI

※

Chiaroscuro - the Italian term meaning "**light and dark**" - is a painting technique that uses light and shadow to create the illusion of light shining on specific objects coming from a particular source. It is, together with linear perspective, what separates medieval art from renaissance art. The effect of this is to give a true sense of three-dimensionality.

※

Another example of his excellent grasp of the art of

chiaroscuro painting occurred when Leonardo's father Piero was asked by one of his favored peasants, a bird-catcher, to have a shield painted that he had made. Piero went to the workshop of Verrocchio and asked Leonardo to paint it. According to Vasari, not only did Leonardo painted a fearsome dragon on it, but, noting that it was poorly made, straightened it over a fire and with a lathe and improved it significantly. Then he painted a fire-breathing dragon in the *chiaroscuro* style on the shield, which was so realistic that when he showed it to his father in an elaborate set-up, dimming the lights and covering the window, he frightened him into thinking that the painting was real. Being the notary that he was, Piero took the shield and sold it to the Duke of Milan for a fortune and purchased another shield to present to the peasant.

❦ VI ❧
WORKING IN MILAN, 1482-99

"It had long since come to my attention that people of accomplishment rarely sat back and let things happen to them. They went out and happened to things."

— LEONARDO DA VINCI

Leonardo went to Milan at the behest of Lorenzo de' Medici (known as Lorenzo the Magnificent), the *de facto* ruler of Florence, as a means of securing peace with the warlike duke, in 1482, and he stayed there until 1499.

The city of Milan was the center of a large and powerful duchy in northern Italy ruled by the powerful Sforza family. It was a part of the Holy Roman Empire at that time and was one of the wealthiest, most artistically diverse places in all of Italy, after Venice and Florence. Having been taught by the noted humanist Filelfo, Ludovico Sforza presided over a renaissance court that was interested in art, science, humanism, and the revival of Greek metaphysics. The architect Donato Bramante arrived in Milan in 1474 and set about designing and overseeing the erection of some churches. The standard Greek grammar book of Constantine Lascaris was printed in 1476 in Milan. Although the musical element of the court was no longer the wonder that it had been under Galeazzo Maria Sforza twenty years earlier when renowned Franco-Flemish composer Josquin des Prez was working there with his group of polyphonic singers, the court of Ludovico still prized music greatly.

ᓚᕙᗩ

Leonardo's time in Milan began with his oft-cited musical performance on the lute he had fashioned out of bronze in the shape of a horse's head. There is very little verifiable information about the early years of Leonardo in Milan (1482-89), leading many to speculate that he was ignored by the powerful duke and his compatriots, leaving him nearly penniless. Of course, they may have only allowed him to pursue his own interests. One of the elements of Leonardo's character that have left many modern critics baffled was his almost total indifference to being paid for his work. He leftcountless commissions unfinished but consequently was rarely paid for his brilliant but unfinished work. This happened in Milan as well.

VII
THE VIRGIN OF THE ROCKS

"The painter has the Universe in his mind and hands."

— LEONARDO DA VINCI

His two most important early commissions in Milan were the two paintings called *The Virgin of the Rocks*, which were commissioned in April 1483 for a dedication in December of the same year by the Confraternity of the Immaculate Conception, and *The Last Supper*, both intended for the monastery of Santa Maria Delle Grazie. *The Virgin of the Rocks* consists of two nearly identical paintings (although only one was requested), along with two side panels depicting angels playing musical instruments.

There was an initial fee of 100 lire paid at the commissioning and a subsequent 40 lire per month until February 1485. This totaled eight hundred lire, and when it was complete, Ambrogio, the other painter requested a further one thousand and two hundred lire but was only given one hundred lire extra. The confraternity had been explicit in what they wanted, and Leonardo had strayed significantly from their request which made them annoyed. As a result, they requested a new painting that would stay close to what they had requested. The confraternity sold the art, and it was lost for many years. Leonardo then set to work on a new version, which was nearly identical except closer to the desires of the confraternity. This was done between 1490 and 1495. It was finally completed and put in place in 1508.

Madonna of the Rocks (left) first version, (right) second version.

VIII
THE LAST SUPPER

"Nothing strengthens authority so much as silence."

— LEONARDO DA VINCI

The Last Supper, the second major commission for Leonardo while in Milan, was left incomplete apparently because he had rendered the twelve apostles so perfectly that he could not imagine how to depict Jesus to look better than the apostles. To the untrained eye, this most famous painting of the renaissance and the most admired and copied painting of all time appears to be completed. However, closer examination reveals that this painting, which probably begun in 1495 covering the wall of the refectory (this was the name for the dining hall) in the monastery and finished around 1497 or 1498, is missing details on its central figure, Jesus. It was to be the centerpiece of the newly-built mausoleum for the Sforza family, and he worked very hard to make the painting perfect, but could not get the face of Jesus correct, and so he left it partly incomplete.

❦

Leonardo was stumped by several issues, the most significant being the face of Judas. He wanted to create the most villainous face possible, and when a prior complained that the painting was taking too long, Leonardo was enraged that he was being questioned, and wrote to the head of the monastery saying that he had been stumped in his search for the most villainous face for Judas but that now he would use the head of the prior who complained.

❦

All twelve apostles have different reactions to the news, just given by Jesus, that he would be betrayed and crucified. Thanks to a recently discovered notebook named "***The Notebooks of Leonardo da Vinci,***" p. 232, we can identify each apostle positively. From left to right, we can identify Bartholomew, Andrew, and James, the son of Alphaeus, grouped together with an expression of surprise. James has both hands up in a gesture of surrender.

❦

In the second group of three, Judas Iscariot, Saul Peter, and John (the beloved) are depicted. Judas, in green and blue, is in shadow, looking as though he were suddenly revealed as the evil man that he is. He is swarthy (which was not considered attractive in the renaissance), and his head is tiny signifying in the renaissance iconography that he was an evil person; he is also holding a bag which may symbolize the pieces of silver he is to be given to betray Jesus, or that notes his role as an apostle of the treasurer. One significant detail is that he is knocking over a salt cellar, which, in the tradition of the time, draws our mind to the concept of "***betraying the salt***," which means that he would betray his master (Jesus). Also noteworthy is the fact that he alone has his elbows on the table, considered a gesture of disrespect. His head is the lowest of anyone in the painting, likewise symbolizing his position as the weakest of the disciples.

❧

Peter, with a white beard, has a look of anger on his face and is holding a knife pointed away from Jesus, foreshadowing his violent reaction to Jesus' arrest, where he cuts off the ear of one of the soldiers arresting Jesus at Gethsemane. John, the beloved, appears to be the youngest of the apostles and is swooning with what must be grief. He is seated at the right hand of Jesus, signifying his favored position in the group of twelve.

❧

Then we have Jesus whose body language creates an equilateral triangle. His turned right cheek is located at what art experts refer to as the vanishing point (the point on the image plane is a perspective drawing where the two-dimensional perspective projections of mutually parallel lines in three-dimensional space appear to converge), making him undoubtedly the focal point in the painting.

❧

Thomas, James (the Greater), and Philip are the next group of three seated to the left of Jesus. Thomas, known in Christian traditions as "***doubting Thomas***" because of his questioning of the resurrection when Jesus returns, is pictured with a quizzical expression and a raised index finger, indicating his doubt. James has an expression of disbelief, with his arms spread wide, looking toward Jesus, and Philip appears to be requesting further explanation of the statements of Jesus.

The final group of three (they are grouped in threes to symbolize the importance of the number three in Christian imagery), consists of Matthew, dressed in ultramarine (the most valuable and expensive color available to the renaissance painter after gold), Jude Thaddeus (in earth tones), and Simon the Zealot. Both Matthew and Jude are turned toward Simon the zealot, as though looking for an explanation.

The painting was initially been imagined as a fresco, to be painted on wet plaster. However, Leonardo, always seeking to outdo his predecessors, applied a double layer of dry plaster over a stone wall, and sealed it with a coat of white lead, upon which he painted the painting using oils and tempera.

The Last Supper has not lasted well through time. As early as 1517, it had been damaged and restored many times, and the image we can see in Milan today is disappointing because much of the original detail has been destroyed. Nevertheless, it remains the most quoted, the most imitated, and the most admired painting of the renaissance, despite the lack of detail on its central figure.

IX
OTHER PROJECTS

"I love those who can smile in trouble..."

— LEONARDO DA VINCI

In the early part of 1485, possibly to avoid the bubonic plague that was ravaging Milan, Leonardo was sent by Ludovico Sforza to Hungary, which had been at war with Milan for many years. Leonardo was sent as a peace ambassador and met with the King of Hungary and Croatia, Matthias Corvinus. He seems to have been successful there, and painted, according to the expert Franz-Joachim Verspohl, a painting of the Holy Family, although the painting in question appears to be lost. He returned to Milan to complete his work on *The Last Supper*, which was completed a few years later.

Although these two commissions have dominated the study of Leonardo's work for many years, he was employed in many other ways by Ludovico Sforza, whose court enjoyed a great deal of artistic display. Leonardo prepared some floats and pageants for special occasions; these pageants, the precursors to operas, were extremely popular and used elaborate sets, stagings, and music.

Leonardo also designed the dome of the Milanese cathedral, and he was the principal builder for a giant equestrian statue that was planned as a tribute to Ludovico's father, Francesco Sforza. In 1492, the clay model of the horse was completed, and it was the largest equestrian monument ever built in Italy. He planned to cast it in bronze and had seventy tons of bronze set aside to make it. The sad postscript to this story is that the seventy tons of bronze were requisitioned to make cannons when the French army alliance collapsed, and when the French invaded and occupied Milan in 1499, the invading soldiers used the clay model of this massive equestrian statue as target practice, destroying it in the process.

1492 was the year the Ludovico allied with the powerful and warlike French King Charles VIII, allowing safe passage for the French army through Milanese territory so that they could attack Naples. Even while Leonardo's younger rival, Michelangelo Buonarotti insulted Leonardo when he suggested that he probably did not know how to cast such a giant statue, Leonardo was, in fact, unable to build it because the bronze was claimed for the making of cannons to defend against the imminent attack by the French army. However, it is doubtful that Leonardo even knew how to cast such a large statue.

※

By 1494, Milan had sided against the French in an attempt to hold back the French forces with alliances with the other Italian states. This ended the alliance and put Milan in jeopardy of being occupied. Of course, ultimately Milan was conquered by the invading French forces in 1499 and was held for many years.

X
HUMAN ANATOMY

"One can have no smaller or greater mastery than mastery of oneself."

— LEONARDO DA VINCI

Another project that Leonardo was involved with while he was in Milan was the accurate rendering of the human anatomy. The philosopher Marc Antonio Delle Torre had dissected a number of corpses and sought out Leonardo to illustrate his work with accurate pen and red ink drawings pictured below.

This endeavor was a significant advance in the field of

anatomy, which had been neglected since the time of Galen of Pergamon in ancient Greece. These accurate drawings of Leonardo debunked many of the mysteries of the human body and many of the incorrect assumptions that had been perpetuated over the centuries. To demonstrate the proportion of the human body he drew the now-famous *Vitruvian Man*. It is so-called because Leonardo was applying his knowledge of the proportions of man based on the writings of the Roman architect Vitruvius in his *De Architectura*. Here is a short translation of some of his work:

※

> *The human body is so designed by nature that the face, from the chin to the top of the forehead and the lowest parts of the hairline, is 1/10th part of the whole height. The open hand from the wrist to the tip of the middle finger is just the same. The head from the chin to the crown is 1/8th, and with the neck and shoulder from the top of the chest to the lowest roots of the hair is 1/6th. From the middle of the chest to the summit of the crown is 1/4. If we take the height of the face itself, the distance from the bottom of the chin to the underside of the nostrils is 1/3 of it. The nose from the underside of the nostrils to a line between the eyebrows is the same; from there to the lowest roots of the hair is also 1/3, comprising the forehead. The length of the foot is 1/6th of the height of the body. The forearm is one quarter, and the breadth of the breast is also a quarter. The other members also have their own symmetrical proportions, and it was by employing them that the famous painters and sculptors of*

antiquity attained to tremendous and endless renown.

❦

In the same way, in the members of a temple, there should be the greatest harmony in the symmetrical relations of the different parts to the general magnitude of the whole. Then, in the human body, the central point is the navel. For if a man is placed flat on his back with his hands and feet extended and a pair of compasses centered at his navel, the fingers and toes of the two hands and feet will touch the circumference of a circle described. And just as the human body outstretched creates a circular outline, similarly a square figure may be found from it. For if we measure the distance from the bottoms of the feet to the very top of the head, and compare that measure to the outstretched arms, the breadth will be found to be the same as the height, like plane surfaces, which are perfectly square.

❦

In his writings on the subject, Leonardo uses a strange backward script that he used for much of what he considered his private papers. Leonardo was primarily left-handed but was considered ambidextrous because he was able to draw with one hand and write with the other. Leonardo also wrote copious notes on the methods he used to paint, also written backward in red ink.

❦

Leonardo planned a work to be completed in 1510-11 that was to include exact and precise reproductions of the human body and all of its organs as well as comparative anatomy (using horses as the comparison).

☙❧

Using his studies of mathematics, optics, mechanics, geology, and botany, he became convinced that motion and force produce all outward forms in nature and give them their shape driven by their function. Informed by the work of earlier scientists, primarily from the Roman period, including Boethius and Cassiodorus, he concluded that objects had their own integrity because of their movement within space.

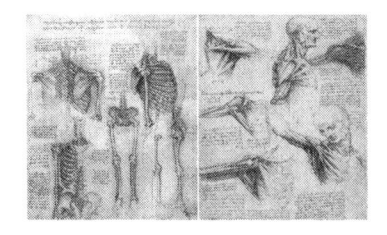

XI
FLIGHT FROM MILAN

"The noblest pleasure is the joy of understanding."

— LEONARDO DA VINCI

After Milan was occupied by the forces of King Charles VIII of France, and the Sforza regime was overthrown, Leonardo and his household, which included the mathematician Lucas Pacioli, removed to Mantua where he began and never finished a portrait of the mighty patroness of the arts there, Isabella d'Este. There remains a series of increasingly annoyed letters from Isabella d'Este in the Leonardo archives, inquiring about the state of her portrait.

Ludovico Sforza, from exile, tried to mount a counter-offensive to drive the French from Milan, which embroiled much of the Mediterranean coast in war with the French, who had superior arms (including the terrifying gun known as the arquebus) and were victorious in nearly every case.

※

Leonardo set out for Venice on the Adriatic Sea. Venice, at this time, was involved in a losing war with the Ottoman Empire (modern-day Turkey); Leonardo found that he was able to find work as a military naval engineer, developing innovative weaponry. He went before the powerful Senate of Venice to propose several novel naval ideas including a floating dam that would draw the Ottoman forces into battle in the Isonzo River. His plan included flooding the Isonzo River valley and installing his floating dam. He also developed a kind of scuba diving contraption that would allow the Venetian forces to mount an underwater attack wherein the soldiers would drill holes in the Turkish boats from the underside. In modern times, these plans, which he kept secret, were built and found to work effectively, but the Venetians saw his ideas as outlandish and did not adopt them.

※

Leonardo, frustrated by their lack of vision, decided to return to Florence. It had been ruled for that past few years by the mad cleric Girolamo Savonarola, who was famous for what is now known as the "***bonfires of the vanities***." There he had public bonfires where citizens were encouraged to burn books and artworks, causing catastrophic damage to both the reputation of Florence as a place where the arts flourished and to the civic structure. By 1498, Savonarola himself had been burned at the stake by the Roman papal forces, and Florence was returned to the Medici (who were also occupying the papal throne).

❧ XII ❧
RETURN TO FLORENCE

"Nothing can be loved or hated unless it is first understood."

— LEONARDO DA VINCI

When Leonardo returned to Florence in 1500, he was 48 years old and at the height of his powers. He was celebrated by the power elite and seemed able to do anything he wanted. For example, when he discovered that an altarpiece for the Nunziata had been commissioned by the Servite friars and given to the artist known as Filippino, Leonardo mentioned that he would have been happy to do this and so Filippino withdrew and allowed Leonardo to take the commission.

He was then taken in with his entire household into the Friars, but he took an inordinately long time to get started, to the annoyance of the Friars. He did draw a cartoon (a study for the altarpiece) of *Our Lady with St. Anne* (the presumed mother of Mary and grandmother of Jesus) in the company of the infant Jesus, and St. John the Baptist playing with a lamb. This was so beautiful that it attracted crowds for days. Leonardo subsequently took this cartoon with him to France.

When completing the altarpiece, Leonardo painted a portrait of Ginevra, the wife of Amerigo Benci, and abandoned the altarpiece, which went back to Filippino, who died and did not complete it.

֎

Leonardo then painted a portrait of Mona Lisa Gioconda, the wife of Francesco del Giocondo, which he left incomplete for many years, and which is currently in the Louvre in Paris, after he gave it to King Francis I of France. This most famous of Leonardo's paintings, the so-called *Mona Lisa*, is renowned partly for the beauty of its subject, and partly because it was so perfectly rendered. According to the myth, Leonardo regularly entertained her with musicians and clowns to keep her smiling. Leonardo took great care to reproduce her every hair in her eyebrows, the color of her lips as compared to her flesh tone in her cheek, the hollow of her throat which appeared to be pulsing. The rendering of her hands was exquisitely beautiful, and the folds of her gorgeous gown were also perfectly reproduced.

※

Why Leonardo chose the background for the *Mona Lisa* is a bit of a mystery. Although typical of his style, she appears to be outdoors, and he was known to have had her sit indoors. Nevertheless, the vanishing curving road is a symbol of the mystery that is in every person, and the lake and the rocky outcroppings are symbolic of his love for nature and the freedom inherent in the painting.

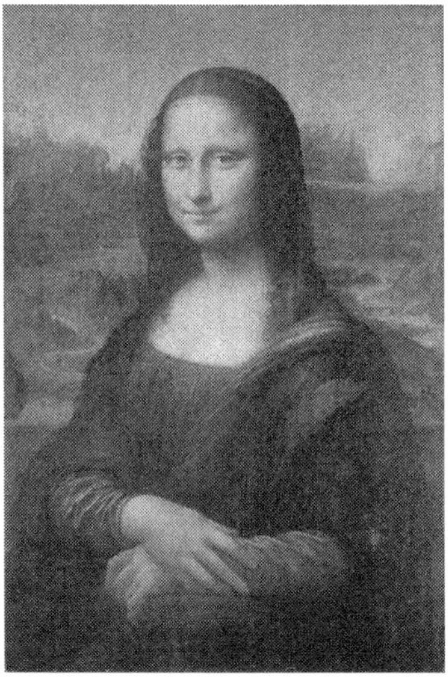

❧ XIII ❧
MILITARY ENGINEER
FOR CESARE BORGIA
(1502-03)

"The smallest feline is a masterpiece."

— LEONARDO DA VINCI

෴

Cesare Borgia, the son of the Borgia Pope Alexander VI, was known as the most corrupt pope in a very corrupt papacy, was of Aragonese descent. He was the favorite illegitimate son of Alexander VI and was made Duke of Valentinois and a cardinal and was the brother of the infamous Lucrezia Borgia. He is also the prince that Niccolo Machiavelli used as a model for a brilliant ruler in his excellent work *The Prince* (*Il Principe*). He was the first person to resign his cardinal in history and became head of the papal forces in Rome and the Papal States at a critical time in Italian history when the French occupied most of Italy. Rome was allied with the

French at the time, and Cesare Borgia at the head of the army of the Papal States entered Milan at the head of the French forces in 1499.

❦

Pope Alexander VI decided that he wanted his illegitimate son (whom he referred to as his nephew, which is where the term nepotism, from the Italian term "***nipote***" meaning nephew, comes from) to have a territory of his own to rule. Accordingly, he declared that the corrupt Papal states of Romagna and Marche were now under his control. The citizens of these states, long abused by their rulers, welcomed this change and Cesare was viewed at the time as a kind and fair ruler.

❦

Cesare Borgia then assumed control of the Papal forces which included a large number of Italian mercenaries, three hundred cavalries and four thousand Swiss infantry who were provided by the King of France. With these forces, he conquered Imola and Forli, and then held by Caterina Sforza. With this victory under his belt, he returned Rome as a conquering hero. He was given the title Papal Gonfalonier by his father.

❦

He continued to Rimini where he defeated Pandolfo Malatesta. Then he conquered Faenza, capturing its leader Astorre III Manfredi, drowning him in the Tiber River. With the help of Florentine forces, he returned to Piombino where he was laying siege to the town. This siege continued until 1502.

Borgia, a brilliant tactician, commanded the French forces in the attacks of both Naples and Capua. He successfully stormed Capua on June 24, 1501, which led to the collapse of the Aragonese power in southern Italy.

※

Cesare Borgia tried to hire Leonardo as his chief military engineer in 1500 to help in his conquest of Pesaro, then ruled by the first husband of his sister Lucrezia Borgia. However, Leonardo was busy with many Florentine commissions and could not take time off until October 1502, when Borgia hired him as his chief military engineer. In this capacity, Leonardo provided Leonardo with an unlimited pass to inspect anything he thought needed attention. Leonardo built the canal from Cesena to the Porto Cesenatico before wintering in the small town of Imola.

※

At Imola, it is believed that Leonardo encountered Niccolo Machiavelli, the great philosopher. While he was in Imola, he drew the first aerial map of a city, which led to the practice in future years.

※

Borgia then marched north, capturing Urbino and Camerino. When he continued to Bologna, some of his troops rebelled, attempting to turn the citizens of Urbino and Camerino against him, but the citizens viewed the rule of Cesare Borgia as the best they had had in many years, and so they rebelled against the rebels, consolidating Borgia's power. Leonardo had left the employ of Cesare Borgia though by this time, and he returned to Florence.

※

Borgia's father, Alexander VI, died in August 1503.Cesare Borgia's power was entirely dependent upon the goodwill of the pope, and the new Pope, Pius III, was not as big a supporter of Borgia's conquests.He was planning a conquest of Tuscany when news of the death of the new Pope arrived. Giuliano Delle Rovere, a mortal enemy of the Borgias, and in particular of Cesare, succeeded Pius III as Julius II.

※

Cesare Borgia, in a weakened position after years of war, tried to make peace with the new pope, but was betrayed when Julius II took power. Ferdinand II of Aragon, still stung by the many defeats in the Italian subcontinent, recruited Gonzalo Fernandez de Cordoba, an erstwhile ally of Cesare Borgia, to imprison Cesare Borgia in Naples. In 1504, Borgia was moved to Spain and imprisoned in the Castle of Chinchilla de Montearagon in La Mancha. When Borgia attempted to escape, he was moved north to the Castle of La Mota, Medina del Campo. Here he escaped and moved through Santander, Durango, and Gipuzkoa; he arrived in Pamplona on December 3, 1506. Here he was received by King John III of Navarre, who hired him as a military commander, fearing an invasion by Castile.

※

Borgia recaptured Viana in Navarre, but although he laid siege to the castle, could not capture it. Some of the knights in the castle escaped and were chased by Borgia, who was left alone. The knights, discovering that he was unable to fight them off due to his army having abandoned him, was ambushed and speared. These knights, enraged by Borgia's success, stripped him and stole his valuables, including the half mask he wore to cover his disfigurement from syphilis and left him to die with a single red tile to cover his genitals.

❧ XIV ☙
THE BATTLE OF ANCHIARO

"Art is never finished, only abandoned."

— LEONARDO DA VINCI

❦

The City of Florence was enamoured with the work of Leonardo at the time, and he enjoyed great success as a painter. The notables in the city met to discuss how best to make use of Leonardo's exceptional talent and decided to hire him to paint. He was commissioned to paint the Great Hall of the Council and began work by creating a cartoon (a study for the final painting) in the Hall of the Pope, which depicted *The Battle of Anghiari* of 1440, which, in turn, depicted Niccolo Piccinino, a commander fighting for Duke Filippo of Milan, with a group of cavalry officers fighting for possession of a standard. The companion piece that was to hang opposite it in the Great Hall, The Battle of Cascina, also a cartoon, was created by Leonardo's nemesis, the great painter and sculptor - Michelangelo Buonarotti.

ঔঞ্জ

This drawing was considered by those who viewed it to be a wonder because of the treatment of the figures in retreat. These figures and their horses show many of the emotions of the defeated including anger and frustration, fear and bitterness to a remarkable degree. One particular figure is trying to snatch the standard, and his shoulder muscles are so accurately depicted that he appears to be able to take it from four horsemen. At the same time, two soldiers are defending the standard while trying to cut the staff with their swords. An older soldier, wearing a red beret seems to yell while grasping the standard with one hand and waving a curved sword with the other hand and attempting to cut off the hands of two others who can be seen to gnash their teeth. Two other soldiers are engaged in hand to hand combat between the legs of the horses, while another man lies on the ground with another on top of him, with a dagger in his arm to stab the man on the ground in the throat.

Also, there are two disproportionately small figures fighting each other on the ground between the horses' legs, while a man lying on the ground has another soldier on top of him; this soldier has his arm raised with a dagger, ready to plunge it into his opponent's throat. This sort of *in medias res* artwork was novel for the time and was received with great enthusiasm. Of course, as was typical of Leonardo at this time, this work was never completed and has since been lost. The reproduction seen above is a copy. The detail though in this work is remarkable as Leonardo, having worked on the largest equestrian statue ever built, had a better understanding of the anatomy and physiognomy of horses than any of his contemporaries. Consequently, his depiction of this battle was better and more perfectly detailed than anything anyone had ever seen.

To paint the final painting on the wall, Leonardo devised a kind of retractable scaffolding that could be raised and lowered at will. Despite the ingeniousness of this design, the wall was so high that when Leonardo began to paint it in oil on top of a new technique called encaustics which was intended to provide depth to the painting. This technique consisted of heating beeswax and allowing it to dry, providing contour on top of the painting.

Setting up braziers near to the painting, Leonardo tried to keep the painting surface warm so that he could apply the oil paint, but this resulted in the oils running and causing the art to be smeared and smudged. When he applied a layer of oil paint, a medium that was still being perfected at the time, the oils, which he had created incredibly thickly to depict depth and contour, began to run and ruined the painting. As a result of this, Leonardo abandoned the painting, and it was never completed.

Despite the catastrophe that the painting became, Piero Sonderini, his patron in this endeavor, continued to pay him every month. When rumors that Leonardo was bilking Sonderini arose, Leonardo attempted to return the money to him, but the latter refused.

❧ XV ❧
SOJOURN IN MILAN
(1506-08)

"As a well spent day brings happy sleep, so life well used brings happy death."

— LEONARDO DA VINCI

❧

Leonardo returned to Milan, the city of his most significant challenges, in 1506, and began work on another equestrian statue, this one to honor the acting French governor of Milan, Charles II Ambroise.

❧

The other theory about this equestrian statue is that Gian Giacomo Trivulzio, who was marshal of the French army and a bitter foe of Ludovico Sforza, commissioned Leonardo to sculpt his tomb in the form of an equestrian statue to be placed in the mortuary of the church of San Nazaro Maggiore in Milan.

꘎

Although it was never completed, there is a wax model that may be authentic, and if it is, then it would be the only extant example of Leonardo's sculpture. He did not stay long in Milan because he was called back to Florence to deal with his father's estate. His father had died in 1506, and although Leonardo was his most accomplished offspring, he was illegitimate and his many brothers and sisters, who were legitimate, created an awful lot of work for Leonardo. However, he returned to Milan in 1508, living in his own house in Porta Orientale in the parish of Santa Babila.

꘎

Although, by all evidence, Leonardo did very little in the way of art during his second time in Milan because he seemed to have been involved with mathematics, he did draw up plans for a palace-villa for King Charles VIII in Milan, and also drew up sketches and plans for an oratory for the church of Santa Maria Alla Fontana, funded by King Charles VIII. His good relationship with King Charles VIII was more important than his works, which would stand him in good stead in his later years. Leonardo was also a consultant on a plan to link Lake Como to Milan via the Adda River (and a series of canals).

꘎

In Milan, he was admired widely and accumulated a large

number of students and followers, including Bernardo de' Conti and his long-time friend and assistant, Gian Giacomo Caprotti, known as Salai (meaning "***little dirty one***").He also had some new students in his studio, including Cesare da Sesto, Giampetrino, and Bernardino Luini. His companion for the rest of his life, Francesco Melzi, a young nobleman, with whose family Leonardo stayed, also entered his life in Milan.

XVI
ROME (1513-16)

"Learning never exhausts the mind."

— LEONARDO DA VINCI

After the death of Cesare Borgia, and the subsequent distaste with all associated which were seen with him, Leonardo suddenly found himself in a very uncomfortable position in Italy. He had to leave Milan in 1513 because of the expulsion of the French forces with whom he had found favor. Consequently, he went to Rome in 1513 with Duke Giuliano de' Medici upon the election of Giovanni Lorenzo de' Medici, the second son of Lorenzo the Magnificent in 1513, as Pope Leo X, hoping to find patronage with Giuliano de' Medici.

Giuliano de' Medici gave him a suite of rooms in the Belvedere, along with a hefty monthly stipend with no commissions to fulfill. In this capacity, he was free to invent things as he saw fit. As a result, Leonardo developed a paste out of a wax which he used to manufacture a kind of balloon material which he used to create inflatable animals that he sent off into the air.

In the garden of the Belvedere where he was living, he found a lizard which he used to create a dragon. He attached some wings with glue that he made from scales scraped from other lizards, and artificial eyes, horns, and a beard. He kept this creature in a box to terrify his friends. Also, Leonardo created a bladder that, when filled with air, would fill up an entire room. As useless as this invention seemed to be, he attracted widespread notoriety in Rome. He also painted a few small commissions but could not secure anything that was long term.

Michelangelo Buonarotti (1475-1564), the celebrated younger painter and sculptor from Florence was in fierce competition with Leonardo, although there is little evidence that Leonardo felt any compunction to compete with Michelangelo. Nevertheless, Michelangelo felt the need to leave Florence and travel to Rome with Duke Giuliano de' Medici and was commissioned to create a facade of San Lorenzo in Florence, causing Leonardo to decide to leave the country for France in 1516, where he spent the remaining years of his life. Interestingly, Michelangelo made a wooden sculpture of this facade but never completed it.

XVII

MICHELANGELO AND LEONARDO

"The knowledge of all things is possible"

— LEONARDO DA VINCI

There was considerable animosity between Leonardo and Michelangelo for most of the latter part of Leonardo's life. Why there was such antipathy between them is a bit of a mystery. According to Vasari, there was an interaction between the two of them that happened in this way, after Leonardo returned to Florence following his attempt to make the colossal equestrian statue in Milan.

Leonardo was walking along the street when he encountered

some friends who were discussing the work of Dante. One of the friends saw Leonardo and, knowing him to be a brilliant mind, asked him to explain it. Leonardo began to explain this but saw Michelangelo and said,

"Michelangelo will tell you what it means."

Like Leonardo, Michelangelo was also a polymath, as well as a great admirer of Dante's, and yet, instead of answering, he said,

"No! Explain it yourself, you horse-modeler who, unable to cast a statue in bronze, was forced to give up the attempt in shame."

According to *The Notebooks of Leonardo da Vinci*, p. 356, Leonardo blushed and remained silent.

❦

Later, when Michelangelo's *David* was first unveiled, Leonardo, alone among the celebrated painters in Florence, objected to the exposed penis on the huge statue and drew what he described as "***a bronze leaf***" to cover the offending member. And Leonardo's objections were not only noted, but the bronze leaf was added to the statue and remained on it for more than forty years. This came from the man who wrote a treatise called "***On the Penis***" in which he argued against "***covering and concealing something that deserves to be adorned and displayed with ceremony.***"

❦

The fact was that Leonardo was known to be the smartest

man who ever lived, but he did not appear to work hard, and he dressed like a dandy, while Michelangelo was one of the most hardworking artists in history, and no doubt it annoyed him that he had to live his life in the shadow of this great man.Similarly, Michelangelo was an avowed celibate, while Leonardo paraded his handsome followers with indiscretion. Michelangelo was notoriously hard-working, while Leonardo seemed unable to finish anything. But truthfully, the world will never know why these two hated one another so much. They just did.

❦ XVIII ❦
FINAL YEARS

"The greatest deception men suffer is from their own opinions."

— LEONARDO DA VINCI

※

Michelangelo left Florence on account of this rivalry and traveled to Rome when Duke Giuliano gave him leave and when he was summoned by the pope to discuss the painting of the facade of the basilica of San Lorenzo in Florence. Hearing of this, Leonardo left and went to France, where the young King Francis I, who owned several of his works, was very fond of him and wanted Leonardo to paint a cartoon of Saint Anne, but, in his habitual manner, Leonardo put the king off with promises.

Because of the popularity and consequent great influx of wealth into the Vatican as a result of the sale of indulgences, which ultimately led to the beginnings of the Protestant faith, Rome saw a vast flowering of art and architecture. Donato Bramante had been hired to build St Peter's Basilica, Michelangelo was working on the tomb of Julius II, while Raphael was painting the rooms in the Pope's apartments. Many other younger artists were taking and finishing many commissions, but these eluded Leonardo, now in his sixties. He was busy of course, working on his scientific studies and inventing things, but he did not receive any of the auspicious commissions, and his letters of the time reveal his frustration at this. He drew a great map of the Pontine Marshes, but otherwise, he was relatively inactive as an artist.

He received an offer from the young King Francis I of France, and in the late fall of 1516, he left Italy forever. He took up residence near the summer palace in Cloud with the title of ***"Premier painter architected et mechanizing du Roi"*** (principal painter, architect, and mechanic to the King).

Although he was primarily involved with his written works, Leonardo did create plans for a residence for the Queen Mother at Romorantin, including a beautiful garden, although the building of this magnificent residence was stopped when an outbreak of malaria threatened the area.

Leonardo prepared much of his treatise on painting, and his work entitled *Visions of the End of the World or Deluge*. In it, he described the primal forces of nature that cause cataclysms for humans.

※

When he died, he received Catholic Last Rites and confessed. He was comforted by the King and died in his arms. He was buried at Cloux, which was devastated during the French Revolution. His grave has been lost.

※

Leonardo is one of only a handful of artists whose reputation has never dwindled throughout history. Although there are only a few verifiable paintings that can be accurately attributed to him, he was acknowledged as the master of the High Renaissance style, and remains as one of the most admired, imitated, and parodied artists of all time.

❧ XIX ❦
LEONARDO'S VERIFIABLE PAINTINGS

"I have been impressed with the urgency of doing. Knowing is not enough; we must apply. Being willing is not enough; we must do."

— LEONARDO DA VINCI

※

1. Annunciation. Leonardo was surely responsible for the background and likely painted, if not all, most of the foreground and the figures in it.

2. Portrait of Ginevra de Benci. Although the authorship of this painting is questionable, many attributes it as the work of Leonardo's hand. The sfumato style, achieved through his unique style of oil painting, suggests his hand, and the tree framing the subject's head is a juniper (in Italian "*ginevra*" a pun on the subject's name), which is a common part of his witty style.

3. Benois Madonna Long believed lost, this painting was only verified in 1909.

4. Adoration of the Magi. This unfinished work is considered to be a masterpiece. It captures both the two elements that are of most importance to a good painter, according to Leonardo: the subject and the subjects' state of mind.

5. Saint Jerome. Like many other Leonardo works, this painting was assumed lost for many years until it was found, in two pieces, by Napoleon's uncle, Joseph Cardinal Fesch. The portrayal of the wild St Jerome with finely muscled arms and a perfectly executed head, surrounded by wild beasts including the first known realistic portrayal of a lion, is far ahead of its time.

6. Madonna of the Rocks.

7. Portrait of a Musician

8. Lady with an Ermine - This relatively simple portrait depicts Cecilia Gallerani, mistress to Ludovico Sforza. The animal is an ermine, the species of weasel whose fur, which in European royalty is favored to be used in their robes. The animal and the hands are rendered with masterful touches.

9. The Last Supper

10. La Sala Delle Asse this painting is unlike any other by Leonardo. Presented with a room to paint while he was busy depicting *The Last Supper*, this room was lost for many years and poorly restored. However, Greenery spreads throughout the ceiling of this great painted room ("*sala*" means "*room*" in Italian) with a single knotted ribbon running throughout which contains his signature - "*Vinci*"

- meaning "*knot*." This painting is similar to many of his drawings in his notebooks.

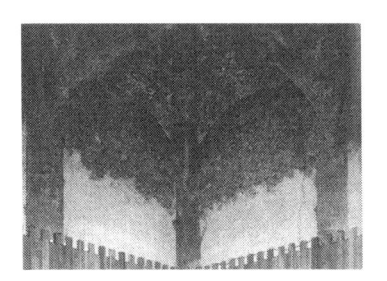

11. Virgin and Child with St. Anne. Another incomplete picture, this painting depicts Mary bending to pick up her child, with her mother, St Anne.

12. Battle of Anghiari. Although Leonardo's original version of this painting is deteriorated due to climate and time, many people, including Rubens, painted copies of it. Its raw violence is reminiscent of Picasso's *Guernica*, painted many centuries later.

13. Saint John the Baptist (1513-16). This is one of Leonardo's last paintings, and it is his least well-known one. The androgynous look of John has perplexed critics for years.

14. Mona Lisa.

15. Salvator Mundi. On November 16, 2017, *Salvator Mundi* was sold at Christie's Auction house in London for 400 million American dollars. This is particularly surprising since it is a peculiar work, only recently authenticated, and of relatively poor quality as what Leonardo paintings go. It is painted in oils on walnut wood, depicting Jesus who appears to be oddly transgendered, wearing clothing that could be masculine or feminine, and giving the sign of peace with his right hand and holding a glass orb in his left.

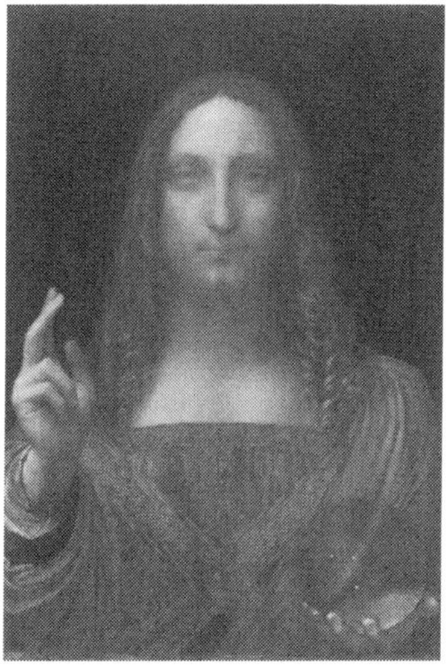

❦ XX ❧
LEONARDO'S PRIVATE LIFE

"There are three classes of people: those who see. Those who see when they are shown. Those who do not see."

— LEONARDO DA VINCI

࿇

Although relatively little is known of Leonardo's private life, it is true that on the eve of his twenty-fourth birthday, he was arrested for the crime of sodomy. This was a serious crime at the time because it had become so prevalent in Florence. So much so that the slang term for a gay person in fifteenth-century German was a "***Florenzer.***" And Leonardo was one of four men secretly accused of having sexual relations with the seventeen-year-old son of a prominent gold merchant. It is not known for how long - if at all - he spent in prison at this time, but it certainly curtailed his activities for two years. Almost nothing is known of his work or his whereabouts in the period following his acquittal for lack of witnesses. Nevertheless, Vasari notes that Leonardo had a practice of buying birds in the market and setting them free, which may have been inspired by his near imprisonment. Also, at this time, or shortly after, he devised two machines: the first was meant to "***open the prison from inside***" and the second was to pry the bars off of windows. It doesn't take a psychologist to see that he was traumatized by this accusation. Nor does it take a savant to know that Leonardo preferred the company of men.

※

Many of his male subjects were particularly feminine or at least appeared to be gender fluid. And of course, there was the second charge, also dropped, of sodomy.

※

Leonardo's notebooks - which contain more than three thousand pages, and an equal number have been lost over the years, reveal much about his mind at work but almost nothing of the man himself. The revelation is that he was unendingly interested in the world around him. He tried to understand the workings of the human body, the atmosphere, bird flight, and innumerable other things that had been opaque to people in the renaissance before him.

※

Despite the many things he explored, he seemed almost completely uninterested in his own psychology. Perhaps this is attributable to his near imprisonment, and maybe it isn't, but it reveals a polymath who lacks a certain introspection. Except this, he was inordinately interested in the androgynous – Dan Brown suggests, in his mega-selling *The da Vinci Code,* one of the apostles was actually and apparently a woman (this, of course, is false, it is John, the beloved, who is exceptionally feminine). Added to this is the revelation, in the 1990s, of a long-lost pornographic image of an angel with breasts and an erect penis. Of course, this in itself reveals little about the great man. Many people have doodled penises, and few of them would feel that this is anything more than a little fun. But this is Leonardo that we are talking about. Known to be illegitimate, left-handed (which was considered suspect to the point that the Italian word for left is "***sinistra***"), vegetarian at a time when almost nobody was, and often heretical in his thought, particularly where religion is concerned. Many have pointed out that he spent an inordinate amount of time and energy in churches and painting or drawing religious subjects. Of course, the reason for this has little or nothing to do with his creative urges; he was fulfilling commissions that were almost invariably for the church.

※

Leonardo was, according to many contemporary reports, extraordinarily attractive. He was effeminate as a youth (as many youths are) and even into his old age, he dressed in a dandyish manner, favoring beautiful pink and purple robes and capes of satin and velvet, and scented his hands with lavender. Vasari also claims that Leonardo was very strong ("***able to bend an iron knocker as though it were made of lead***"), which only feeds this superhuman mystique.

***

The fact that he was illegitimate was not a cause for embarrassment, but it did save him from following his father into the family business. Instead, he was free to choose his profession - although it was his father, a good friend of Verrocchio - who approached the master and asked that he train Leonardo. Similarly, his lack of formal education, which could have been a huge detriment to his life had he been less energetic as an autodidact, was a benefit to him, allowing him to discover whatever he wanted, whenever he wanted. Sometimes, of course, this sort of freedom leads a young man into trouble. So it did with Leonardo.

***

Much to the consternation of many biographers, Leonardo, a renaissance man in every conceivable way, was gay. He had a lover whom he lived with openly (or as openly as a man can live) but whom he described in his notebooks as "*a thief, a liar, obstinate, greedy.*" That liar, thief, who was obstinate and greedy was Gian Giacomo Caprotti, a man who came into his household as a ten-year-old boy in 1490. Caprotti entered his workshop to learn the art of painting, and was extraordinarily attractive, "*with lovely curling hair which Leonardo adored,*" according to Vasari. He was as often a model as a painter and served mainly as a servant.

***

This boy stayed with Leonardo for twenty-eight years and later had a reasonably good career as a painter. Leonardo used him as a model for some of his angels. However, he was also a thief and stole purses, pens, and almost anything else of value, and so Leonardo gave him the nickname Salaì, which translates to "***dirty little devil***," more or less, and that is the name which he is known in his artwork. It is clear that Salaì was his lover; although he did not age particularly well, he seems to have charmed Leonardo from when he was fifteen and well into his adulthood. The most enduring image of Salaì is a light sketch of his face surrounded by a heart.

※

Of course, Leonardo was gay - his only childhood memory is of a bird - a kite - flying down to his cradle, and putting his tail into Leonardo's mouth, "***past the lips***" as he phrased it. Sigmund Freud, many years later, described this memory as corresponding to the act of fellatio, an idea that enraged many critics at the time, but something that would surprise exactly nobody today.

※

But Leonardo's interest in the idea of the transgender and his *Salvator Mundi* is often cited as an evident attempt to degender Christ and portray him as either transgender or sexless were brought to light in a strange drawing discovered in 1991, depicting an angel sporting both breasts, and a rather large erection (with the pointless erasure marks that show that he did not want this discovered). It has been suggested that this drawing was part of a much larger, and a much hidden cache of secret pornographic Leonardo drawings that were stolen in the nineteenth century prompting relief to the heteronormic world of the nineteenth century.

※

His *Last Supper* was painted directly on to the wall in Milan in the room that was to be Ludovico 'il moro' Sforza's tomb. It is believed that he did this because he did not want it to be taken away by the French, who, even in 1495, were threatening to invade. He painted it directly on the wall, which necessitated the technique of fresco, which meant that by 1517 it was already flaking off the wall. Leonardo knew about this and was concerned.

ॐ

Leonardo was one of the slowest painters in all of art history - less than twenty of his paintings survive - and he liked to think hard about his work. The result is that his work is singularly well-thought and through, and yet despite this slow pace, even some of his attributed paintings were incomplete. This incompleteness is one of Leonardo's most interesting attributes. Much of his life, even though he clearly wanted to leave the world with his most profound thoughts, is a mystery to the modern observer.

❧ XXI ☙
HOW CAN WE USE LEONARDO'S STRENGTHS IN OUR LIVES?

"It is easier to resist at the beginning than at the end."

— LEONARDO DA VINCI

☙❧

Leonardo was a man consumed by the desire for learning; he claimed that hard work tamped down sensuousness, and he left the world with some of the most profound thoughts ever recorded. He carried with him a notebook at all times so that he could record his ideas, which almost always were a consideration, brilliantly thought through, of the world around him. While he created machines of war in significant numbers, he seems to have been a man of peace. Working for the bloodthirsty Cesare Borgia, he confined his work to inspecting the fortifications and was clearly revolted by the bloodlust of this young prince. He only lasted eight months. Leonardo had his standards, and nothing could shake him from these beliefs.

※

Although he spent a lot of time in and around churches and people of faith, he was not a devout Catholic, as many of his contemporaries were. He was a man of science, and the scientific world, especially in the high renaissance, was often at odds with the teachings of the church. One has only to think of the troubles of Copernicus and Galileo to know that this was an area of great discomfort for the thinking man. And yet, Leonardo had little nuisance with the church, as many of his more devout contemporaries did. By all accounts, except the crude and rude Michelangelo, he seems to have been able to get along with others in a way that is enviable even in a mild-mannered accountant. He possessed great physical strength but was loath to use it. He was brilliantly talented at music, at painting, at sciences, at architecture and the arts of war, and yet he seems to have been extraordinarily modest as well, despite his propensity for fancy clothes and fancy accommodations.

※

Leonardo's great load was hidden beneath a bushel, and he used this modesty to make sure that he was appreciated. He alone among the great painters of the renaissance was admired during his life, and continuously after. This ability to show a clear understanding of his place in the universe was one of his best qualities. Although he lived at a time of great division - the mad theocracy of Girolamo Savonarola, the conquests of Charles VIII and Cesare Borgia, the changing place of many people in society, the expulsion of the Jews from Spain, many of whom went to northern Italy, establishing the banks that made northern Italy the wealthiest place on earth for many centuries, the discovery of America, which thrilled many Europeans, and many other innovations, he seems to have taken these many changes in stride, looking with clear eyes at the situation and navigating it with sensitivity and aplomb. This ability to function in a rapidly changing world is a quality we can take and apply to our rapidly changing world.

※

It is said that Leonardo knew all that was to know in the renaissance. As hyperbolic as this seems, it may have actually been true, judging by the incredible contributions he made to art, to science, and to many other areas. He drew sketches of parachutes, submarines, all kinds of fearsome implements of war, dams, scuba gear, airplanes and helicopters, armoured car, tank, barrel organ for firing guns much more quickly, anemometer (an instrument to measure the speed of wind), more accurate clock, self-propelled cart, robotic knight, and the world's first revolving bridge. This astonishing list is even more surprising because almost none of these inventions was ever even built. Sure, many of his designs did not work, but many more of them did work as the exhibit by the Library of Congress from 2003 demonstrated, when they built the machines and showed how effective they would have been if they had been built in his time.

※

Leonardo was a man of his time - he sought out patronage, which meant that he also had to cultivate a modest and kind demeanor, which he did better than any other artist of his time. He had innumerable patrons who made little or no demands on his time and energy to create. Like modern thinkers, he did not feel that it was necessary to continually create new things to prove his value in society. Instead, he cultivated friends of all social strata from the thief to the king. He knew most of the most influential people in Europe at the time from Lorenzo "**the Magnificent**" de' Medici to Ludovico "***il moro***" Sforza, Cesare Borgia, several popes, King Charles VIII of France and Francis I of France, Niccolo Machiavelli, as well as many other nobles too numerous to list. He was also well acquainted with the lowest people in society, and sixty beggars followed his casket to its final resting place as stipulated in his will.

※

He was a good and true friend, never treating any of his closest friends with anything but the greatest generosity. Vasari claims that he was the perfect human ever created, and although he was gay at a time when it was both frowned upon and scandalous, he seems to have had little or no trouble leading an out-gay lifestyle. He was a brilliant musician and singer, orator, writer, scientist, painter, sculptor, and architect. If any of us could match Leonardo in only one of his many disciples, we would be justifiably self-satisfied.

❦ XXII ❧
ADDITIONAL READING LIST

❦

- Isaacson, Walter, *Leonardo da Vinci*, Simon and Shuster, 2017
- Bramly, Serge, *Leonardo: The Artist and the Man*, Penguin Books, 1988, translated by Sian Reynolds
- Charles Nicholl, *Leonardo Da Vinci: The Flights of the Mind*, Allen Lane, 2004

YOUR FREE EBOOK!

As a way of saying thank you for reading our book, we're offering you a free copy of the below eBook.

Happy Reading!

GO WWW.THEHISTORYHOUR.COM/CLEO/

Printed in Great Britain
by Amazon